Everything was quiet and peaceful.

Then Joe started clicking his fingers. Clickety click!

4

Josh started tapping the table. Tappity tap!

Tara hit her chair.

Bang-banga! Bang-banga!

Tomas made sounds with
his mouth. Tuck-tucka!
Tuck-tucka!

Ravi patted his knees.

Pat-pata! Pat-pata!

Gloria shook her pencil
case. Rattle rattle!
Rattle rattle!

"Hmm, hmm!" hummed Jay.
"Hmm, hmm!" hummed Jenna.

And they clapped their
hands together.
Patapat! Patapat!

12

"Who," said Mr Edwards, "is making all that noise?"

Mr Edwards looked
at everyone.

"Right, all of you! I want to see you later!"

15

So later they all waited
outside Mr Edwards' room.

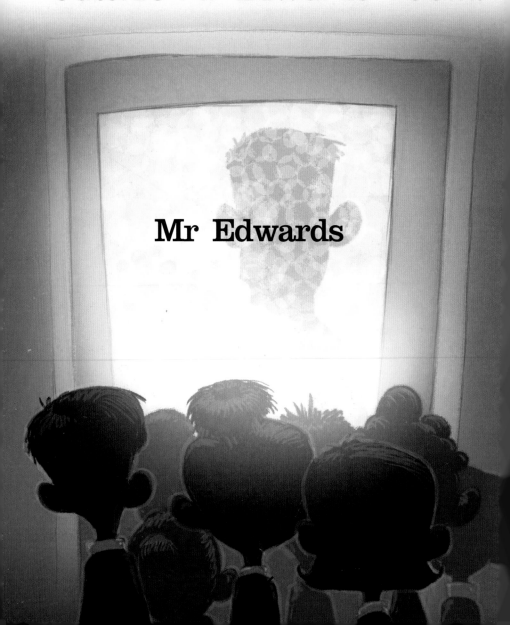

Mr Edwards

"Come in," said Mr
Edwards. He was smiling!

Everyone stared.
There were so
many drums!

Mr Edwards

"Want to learn?"
asked Mr Edwards.

They played those drums
and bells and shakers.

They played until the sound was just right.

Then they played in front of everyone!

They played the small
drums. "Pat, patta!
Pat, patta!"

They played the big
drums. "Dum a dum,
dum a dum!"

They made those iron
bells ring. "Ding ding!
Ding ding ding!"

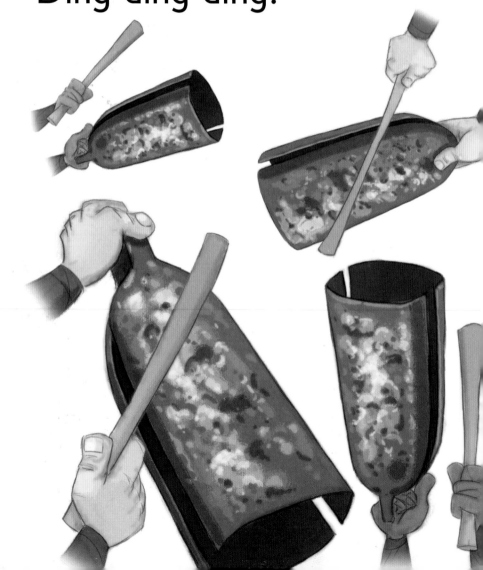

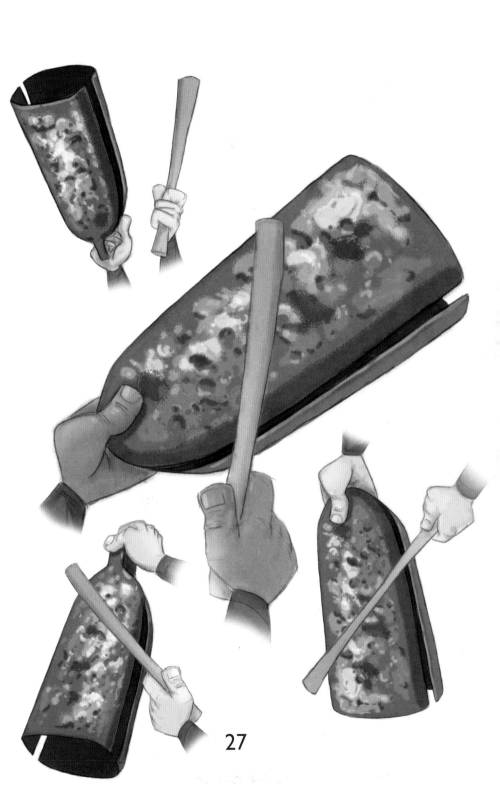

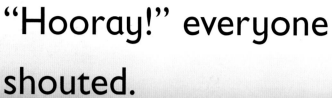

"Hooray!" everyone shouted.

"We just **love** that noise!"

Puzzle 1

a

b

c

d

e

f

Put these pictures in the correct order.
Now tell the story in your own words.
How short can you make the story?

angry   pleased

proud

excited   happy

miserable

Choose the words which best describe each character. Can you think of any more? Pretend to be one of the characters!

Answers

Puzzle 1

The correct order is:

1d, 2e, 3a, 4f, 5b, 6c

Puzzle 2

Mr Edwards The correct words are pleased, proud.
The incorrect word is angry.

Ravi The correct words are excited, happy.
The incorrect word is miserable.

Look out for more Leapfrog stories:

For details of all our titles go to: www.franklinwatts.co.uk

*hardback